ST

*R. S. Thos*

# Strangely Orthodox

## *R. S. Thomas*
## *and his Poetry of Faith*

Barry Morgan

Gomer

To Hilary
for all the love and support

Published in 2006 by
Gomer Press, Llandysul, Ceredigion SA44 4JL
www.gomer.co.uk
Second Impression 2006

ISBN 1 84323 682 6
ISBN-13 9781843236825
A CIP record for this title is available from the British Library

This book is published with the financial support of the
Welsh Books Council.

Printed and bound in Wales at
Gomer Press, Llandysul, Ceredigion

# Contents

# Foreword

by

# The Archbishop of Canterbury

Already the literature about R. S. Thomas is swelling to immense proportions; and no doubt it will continue to do so in the decades ahead. It is, then, all the more important to have some clear and authoritative signposts for understanding him. Barry Morgan has the advantage not only of a full and close knowledge of the poems, but also of a close personal acquaintance with the poet as a priest and preacher.

In this lucid study, Archbishop Barry carefully locates R. S. Thomas against a broad backcloth of theological and spiritual history. Poets do not come from nowhere, even (especially?) poets of the stature of R.S.; here is, not a genealogy or a dull study of 'influences' (like others, I well remember how much R.S. disliked being asked about 'influences'), but a sketch of those voices with which the poet is in constant conversation, voices within and on the edge of the Christian tradition, as he is himself.

This is a deeply helpful and creative guide, to be welcomed not only by the general reader but by the Christian student for whom R. S. Thomas can be a disturbing and unsettling voice. Barry Morgan's closing remarks about how the poet speaks to a generation for which the institution of the church often seems in crisis, yet for whom the echoes of the spirit are powerful, offer a very timely word.

† ROWAN CANTUAR

# Preface

I did not set out to write a book on the poetry of R. S. Thomas. The idea arose out of a quiet day I spent in the company of some of the clergy of the Llandaff diocese at Tymawr Convent, Monmouth. My addresses on that occasion were based on the religious themes of R. S. Thomas's poetry and the then Mother Superior, Sister Gillian, suggested that I ought to consider publishing the substance of what I had said. I have been an admirer of Thomas's poetry since my undergraduate days. I had no means of knowing then that I would get to know him, still less take his funeral and preach at his memorial service. The strength of his poetry for me was his sheer honesty in facing some of the difficulties that believing in God entails. At various moments of crises in my own ministry it was to his poetry I turned for both illumination and sustenance since he was never satisfied with glib, easy answers to complicated questions of faith. I never went away disappointed and this short book for the general reader is meant merely to give a sketch of the main religious themes of his poetry as I see them.

I am enormously grateful to Dr Raymond Stephens, Canon Donald Allchin and Professor Wynn Thomas for their many helpful comments and insights and to my long-suffering secretary, Mrs Avril Paxton, for her patience and expertise in dealing with the production of this work. I am also grateful to Palgrave Macmillan Publishers, Bloodaxe Books and Mr Gwydion Thomas for permission to quote extensively from R. S. Thomas's poetry and to Mrs Betty Thomas for her encouragement.

BARRY MORGAN
ARCHBISHOP OF WALES

# Introduction

When I first met R. S. Thomas, his first wife had just died. I went as his local archdeacon to extend my condolences to him on his bereavement. His response was to say mischievously that he had spent his whole life avoiding people in the church hierarchy like me. He then asked me in, made a cup of tea and we spent a delightful hour chatting about all kinds of things.

He died in September 2000 aged 87. He was arguably the greatest Anglo-Welsh poet of his time but his work has also been translated into many languages, among them Danish, Hebrew, Japanese, Swedish, Italian, French and German, so that he is a poet of world renown. Nominated by the Welsh Academy of Writers [Yr Academi Gymreig] for the Nobel Prize for Literature in 1996, he won the Heinemann Award for poetry in 1955, the Queen's Gold Medal for poetry in 1964, the Cholmondeley Award in 1978, received four Welsh Arts Council literature awards, the Lifetime Achievement Award for Poetry from the Cannon Foundation, Los Angeles in 1996, the Horst Bienek Prize for poetry from the Bavarian Academy of Fine Art and was made a Fellow of the Cymmrodorion Society. He wrote the equivalent of one poem every fortnight for fifty years, more than 1500 poems in all. A priest of the Church in Wales, whose poetry arose from and was shaped by his priesthood, he was, nevertheless, not a man of simple, uncomplicated faith. He shirked none of the hard questions that believing in God entails. As a result his poetry bears the stamp of his inner wrestling with God as he strives to make sense of His purposes in the universe. Thomas's life was a perpetual striving to find meaning amongst the uncertainties of the modern world.

R. S. Thomas was a man full of paradoxes. As a person, he could look fierce, austere, forbidding even and yet could be the gentlest and most sensitive of men in his human relationships. He might look remote and reserved and yet, in conversation, be frank and open. He could appear dour and yet had a delightfully impish sense of humour; he could rail against the anglicisation of his country and yet admire the great English poetic tradition and write poetry (however reluctantly) in English. He married women who spoke no Welsh. He would refuse invitations to go to local comprehensive schools to discuss his poetry since he did not want to add to the dilution of the Welsh language, and yet would consent to give poetry readings at festivals all over the country, though he did not like publicly discussing particular poems. He could make the most provocative and cutting of statements about the English and their Welsh holiday homes, and yet could be personally kind and compassionate. He was a patriotic Welsh Nationalist who sounded so very English. He even educated his son at an English boarding school despite giving him the very Welsh name Gwydion. Sometimes he would claim to love nature more than humanity even though some of his poems about people are full of love and tenderness. He might sometimes give the impression of knowing the names of the birds in his parish better than the names of his own parishioners, yet his poetry shows how keenly he observed those same parishioners with pastoral concern and even love. But he never romanticised or sentimentalised them. He tried to tell the truth about people as he saw them.

Ronald Thomas (he added the Stuart only in adult life) was born in Cardiff in 1913, but from the age of five was brought up in Holyhead. A Classics graduate from University College, Bangor, as it was then called, he did his theological training at St Michael's, Llandaf. In his autobiography *Neb* ('No one'), however, he claimed not to like the South since he did not feel at ease there. Of his time at St Michael's he wrote:

> He derived no pleasure from the return. He soon began to
> yearn for the life and background of the North. There was
> nowhere to go for a walk except along a main road. There
> were no mountains, no open ground. Worse still, the year
> was divided into four terms, which meant that he had to
> return in the middle of the summer to complete the fourth.
> Neither the college nor the routine appealed to him at all.
> After the Hostel in Bangor the buildings were old-
> fashioned, the food uninteresting, the Chapel nothing but
> some prefabricated hut and the Warden effeminate. The
> students did not take the College seriously.      (*As* 41–2)

He wrote that he had not learnt a great deal from the place
and the highpoints of his time there were a recital by the
great violinist Kreisler and a rugby match between Wales
and the All Blacks.

He was ordained in the diocese of St Asaph in 1936
(presumably because at that stage he spoke no Welsh)
although he lived in the predominantly Welsh diocese of
Bangor. He served curacies at Chirk and Hanmer before
becoming in turn Rector of the mid-Wales village of
Manafon in the St Asaph diocese, then Eglwys Fach in the
diocese of St David's. By that time he had learnt Welsh.
Finally he came to be the parish priest of Aberdaron on the
Llŷn peninsula in the diocese of Bangor. He retired at the
age of 65, first to Aberdaron, then Llanfair-yng-Nghornwy
on Anglesey and finally to Pentrefelin near Cricieth. He
married Mildred (Elsie) Eldridge, an artist, whilst curate of
Chirk, and they had one child. In his eighties he married
Betty Vernon, a widow who survives him. He was made an
honorary professor in the Welsh Department at the
University of Wales, Bangor, after his retirement.

He would have liked to have written his poetry in Welsh
– even though it was not the language of the hearth; but by
the time he learnt it, he was 30 and felt, much to his regret,
unable to express himself poetically in it. He harboured a
certain resentment against his mother for not teaching him
the language and perhaps his harsh strictures against the

anglicisation of his country were in part directed towards himself (and against her) for his inability to express his deepest thoughts in Welsh. He published his autobiography *Neb* in Welsh but did not regard prose in the same light as poetry. Influenced by George Steiner's book *After Babel* he believed that to lose the Welsh language was to lose contact with one's own ancestral roots.

Although his poetry arose out of his vocation and ministry as a parish priest, he admitted that in some ways his call to ordination was a bit unusual since he was not, at that time, a regular churchgoer. He also claimed that 'his Mother saw that her son had no strong objection to the idea of being a candidate for Holy orders' (*As* 35), all of which he wryly interpreted as God calling people in mysterious ways. He was, nonetheless, a devoted and devout parish priest. His daily pattern was to spend the morning studying, go for walks in the afternoon and in the evening visit his parishioners since it was no use visiting them in the day when they would be out on the farms working. His earliest poetry portrayed the tough life of his parishioners, peasant upland farmers eking a living from the land. The depth and commitment to his priestly vocation is clear in 'The Priest':

> 'Crippled Soul', do you say? Looking at him
> From the mind's height; 'limping through life
> On his prayers. There are other people
> In the world, sitting at table,
> Contented, though the broken body
> And the shed blood are not on the menu.'

> 'Let it be so', I say. 'Amen and Amen'.          (*CP* 196)

In other poems such as 'Country Cures' (*CP* 124), and 'In Church' (*CP* 180) he speaks of the loneliness and stresses of his priestly vocation. It was not, after all, an easy and untroubled ministry.

In Manafon he tried to write about the people of the country, but at Aberdaron 'he turned increasingly to the question of the soul, the nature and existence of God and the problem of time in the universe' (*As* 76). Writing about himself in the third person he says that 'the religious vein in his poetry became more visible during his last years for after all there is nothing more important than the relationship between man and God' (*As* 104). This might have had something to do with his growing older, or may have been influenced by the fact that Aberdaron was on the pilgrim route to Bardsey Island, reputed to be the place of burial of thousands of saints during the early Celtic Christian centuries. By his own admission, and in spite of all the other subjects he wrote about, he is regarded – as he indeed regarded himself – first and foremost as a religious poet. His poetry grew out of his ministry amongst people and his struggle to apprehend the living God. In this he was like his great Anglican predecessor George Herbert, lines from whose poem 'The Church Porch' were to be found in the hallway of his home:

> When once thy foot enters the church, be bare.
> God is more there than thou; for thou art there
> only by his permission.

The scriptures were his daily diet. That is why in his last radio broadcast a few months before he died, he wanted six passages read from them as well as from Spenser, Hardy, Wordsworth, Eliot, Yeats and Edward Thomas.

In an introduction to the *Penguin Book of Religious Verse*, R. S. Thomas defines religion as the response of the whole person to reality, and poetry as the imaginative presentation of it (*PBR* 9). In one of his poems he writes:

> Poetry is that
> which arrives at the intellect
> by way of the heart.                (*Res* 69)

One's vital emotions must be totally engaged yet controlled by the intellect in a successful poem. It must express, in Wordsworth's striking words, a 'truth carried alive into the heart by passion'.

According to *The Creative Writer's Suicide*, Thomas saw it as his duty to exercise every literary talent he had in order to create a memorable statement in this poetry. He wrote out of an inner compulsion to write but it was at a cost – discipline was required and suffering could follow. Moreover, 'unbeknown to the poet, things sink into the subconscious to form there a matrix or pool from which he can draw at some time in the future. It is in this way that so many successful poems came into being' (*As* 71). For him, writing was a discipline that needed time and silence to ensure receptivity to the heart's deepest promptings.

Whilst some poems could come without much effort or warning, it was not generally the case, since he often writes about the battle and strain of composition. Indeed, in this respect, he often compared writing poetry to an encounter with God. At times it seems to happen without great effort, yet at other times God's presence is felt only after a long period of contemplating and searching. As he himself puts it in 'Kneeling':

> Moments of great calm,
> kneeling before an altar
> Of wood in a stone church
> In summer, waiting for the God
> To speak; the air a staircase
> For silence: the sun's light
> Ringing me, as though I acted
> A great rôle. And the audiences
> Still; all that close throng
> Of spirits waiting, as I,
> For the message.
>                         Prompt me God:
> But not yet. When I speak,

Though it be you who speak
Through me, something is lost.
The meaning is in the waiting.                    (*CP* 199)

God and the poetic impulse do not come to the poet at his
bidding. He must wait. 'The meaning is in the waiting.' God
will speak through the poet when God is ready to do so.

This short book is concerned with some of the themes
which recur in many of his poems. One treads on
dangerous ground in dealing with them for, as he himself
once wrote, 'a poem's message is in itself, one can no
more tear apart form and content in a poem than body and
soul in a human being. The medium is the message' (*WV*
18). I hope that I shall not brutally separate form from
content, the medium from the message in what follows.

*It is this great absence*
*that is like a presence . . .*

# Chapter 1

# The Nature of God

Many people find R. S. Thomas's poetry bleak. There is spareness in both his language and his thought that can prove forbidding. But, believing as he did that the relationship between man and God was the most important there was, he said that there was nothing more difficult and problematic than establishing it, for as he put it 'Who is it who ever saw God? Whoever heard Him speak? We have to live virtually the whole of our lives in the presence of an invisible and mute God. But that was never a bar to anyone seeking to come into contact with Him. That is what prayer is' (*As* 104).

By confronting this question of the elusiveness and absence of God, R. S. Thomas is, of course, reflecting the experience of the modern age. As Bishop John Habgood points out in many of his writings, we live in a de-sacralised universe, where God is not seen as playing an active part in the world – the age of miracles is over and in a world where there is so much evil and destruction, it can be difficult to believe that there is a God, still less a God of love. Yet as Habgood also points out, the fact that God may be felt to be absent is not just a feature of our age – there have always been complaints about the absence of God. Indeed, many of the Psalms address this issue directly, urging the Almighty to demonstrate his presence in the world: 'Lord, why do you hide your face from me' [*Psalm* 88[14]] or 'How long, Lord, will you hide yourself from sight?' [*Psalm* 89[46]].

## The Impossible Definition

To define God, as this poet knew, is impossible. He cannot be so neatly captured. This is why Thomas's major themes are the hiddenness of God, the elusiveness of God, the mystery of God, the silence of God, the darkness of God, and even the absence of God. In examining such themes Thomas showed how steeped he was in Holy Scripture, and in the writings of the Fathers and of Christian mystics. It is interesting that one of his volumes of poetry is entitled *H'm* (1972), and is devoted to probing both the existence and the nature of God. Does the apostrophe in the title indicate the omission of the letter 'i'? Is the volume actually about 'Him', that is God? In the Old Testament, God was never called by his proper name, in order to respect his 'otherness'. He could never be defined by a name and Thomas's enigmatic title might be a reflection on that theology. Christian tradition has always maintained that God is ultimately unknowable as He is in Himself, a mystery to which our human words point only by analogy. Only something that can be fully defined can be proved, and so, since it is impossible to prove the existence of God in the abstract, God remains a concept about the way things are. The possible missing letter in *H'm* points to the ultimate 'unknowability' of God. Thomas accepted the fundamental fact of God's existence and reminds us that He is not an object to be explored, but a mystery in whose presence one can ultimately only rest in faith, hope and prayerful silence. Since God is beyond anything we can directly conceive or understand, it is only through using images, metaphors and analogies that one can begin to find a language for Him, and these elements are always provisional, inadequate and incomplete. One often has to resort to saying what God is not, rather than what He is, and this is what Christian thinkers throughout the ages have always done. 'To whom can God be compared?' asks Isaiah, for 'His thoughts are not our thoughts and His ways not ours' (*Isaiah* 40 v18; 55 v8). As the poet himself said in a radio broadcast, 'it is the attempt to define him – that's when the trouble begins – perhaps we should not attempt to define him.' Indeed 'If the creature can comprehend his creator, his creator is no longer a creator' (*AWR* 39). Not even modern mathematics or the wonders of modern science can pin God down:

> My equations fail
> As my words do. (*CP* 361)

> Genes and molecules
> have no more power to call
> him up than the incense of the Hebrews
> at their altars. (*CP* 361)

God cannot be conveniently summoned or restricted to some holy shrine where man can be sure to find Him, for that would remove the sovereign freedom of God and once more reduce Him to being just one object among other objects in our world.

It is impossible to define God and modern technological man has no more ability to reach Him than his less sophisticated predecessors. For the poet, God is awesome and beyond our reach for no one can read God's mind. So in a memorable image, the poet compares trying to understand God to the way that waves running up the shore always fall back:

> I run
> up the approaches of God
> and fall back. (*MHT* 43)

## The Silence of God

God is so far beyond us and beyond the capacity of our intellects to understand him that all we can often do is be without speech before his silent presence. 'Whose silence so eloquent as His?' the poet asks in 'Nuclear' (*CP* 317).

Yet the paradox is that no nuclear bomb has been as explosive as the Word revealed in Jesus since the fall-out from that has been endless.

In *Counterpoint,* he examines this silence yet further:

> But the silence in the mind
> is when we live best, within
> listening distance of the silence
> we call God. This is the deep
> calling to deep of the psalm-
> writer, the bottomless ocean
> we launch the armada of
> our thoughts on, never arriving.          (*C* 50)

Whilst elsewhere he claims that

> I dwelt
> in a soundless darkness
> in the shadow
> of your regard.          (*CP* 280)

and that

> I listen
> instead and hear the language
> of silence . . .          (*CP* 343)

along with the 'splendour of God's darkness'.

Since 'Silence is God's chosen medium of communication' (*CP* 388), the silent God evokes our silence in turn in his presence so that paradoxically in and through such a silence an encounter between man and God can occur. For as the poet goes on to explain in *Counterpoint*:

> It is a presence, then,
> whose margins are our margins;
> that calls us out over our
> own fathoms. What to do
> but draw a little nearer to
> such ubiquity by remaining still? (*C* 50)

He feels that although there is not a word exchanged, a silent encounter is the best encounter there can be between man and God for in and through it a relationship is forged; a kind of mutual watching is taking place in silence:

> The relation between us was
> silence; that and the feeling
> of each one being watched
> by the other.
>
> (*NTF* 83)

*had the look of being looked at*

*stay calm*
*pay attention*

But this is an active not a passive watching and waiting – an alert kind of attention in God's presence. It is attempting to be still in His presence, as the Psalmist exhorts us to be, and this requires alertness and openness to what God may have to offer. It is about searching the otherness of God and that involves effort and devotion for 'the poet makes his return on his knees' (*MHT* 43). In order to have this relationship with God, one has to turn away from the noise of machines and the materialistic bustle of our world:

> It is a turning aside,
> a bending over a still pool,
> where the bubbles arise
> from unseen depths, as from truth
> breathing.
>
> (*MHT* 34)

God is present in the silence, even though 'no word came' (*CP* 67) as the poet kneels in the silence of a country church. But

> The darkness implies your presence . . .
> It is not your light that
> can blind us; it is the splendour
> of your darkness.
>
> (*CP* 343)

Yet even in silence before God – the poet's silence – there is no guarantee that he will necessarily feel the presence or nearness of God:

There was no admiring
of my restraint, no suggestion even
of a recompense for my patience.
If he had allowed himself but one
word: his name, for instance, spoken
ever so obliquely; my own that,
for all his majesty, acknowledged
my existence.                                    (*NTF* 83)

But the mystery remains. One can only go on waiting 'somewhere between faith and doubt' (*CP* 347), hoping that God will respond by showing 'the ubiquity of a vast concern' (*CP* 353).

## Desire and darkness

The desire for God is a desire of the heart rather than the intellect; knowing God is to have a loving relationship with Him. In this way Thomas echoes the author of the fourteenth-century spiritual treatise *The Cloud of Unknowing* who states, 'that God cannot be reached through the intellect and by reason but through love' – that is through waiting attentively in love for God to reveal himself. In *Counterpoint* Thomas tells of how a migrant bird instinctively flies skywards, without worrying about its destination, and so our souls aspire towards God in a  longing relationship of love for Him. Here he echoes the prayer of St Augustine and the claim that the hearts of people are restless until they find their rest in God. It is a reaching out for God hoping that he might reciprocate in some way, and it is a perfectly natural thing for humans to do. But the poet realises, as the medieval mystic Meister Eckhart did, that 'where understanding and desire end, there is darkness and there God's radiance begins'. So too the seventeenth-century divine Henry Vaughan, who speaks of God's dazzling darkness. In the darkness God is to be found; one has to risk entering it in order to make any headway towards Him for

The darkness
is the deepening shadow
of your presence; the silence a
process in the metabolism
of the being of love.                         (*CP* 296)

The paradox is that this God of silence and darkness is not
absent, but present in and through that very silence and
darkness. The extraordinary thing is that when one enters
that region one sometimes finds not nothingness but
intimations of the presence of the living God. Thus

There are times even at the Pole
when he, too, pauses in his withdrawal
so that it is light there all night long.        (*C* 54)

As a priest, R. S. Thomas would spend a great deal of time
in church where he could find peace and quietness to
cultivate the presence of God or to interrogate Him in
some agony of mind. Kneeling in church he would be met
only by God's silence and in one poem he asks
paradoxically whether the church is the place God hides
from his searching (*CP* 180). He ends the poem rather
bleakly as he tests his faith against the emptiness of
the church and the possibility of an 'untenanted cross'
(*CP* 180).

He comes to the conclusion that it is not so much a
place that is required for stillness to find God but an
attitude of mind and heart in which he might feel that

you are at our shoulder, whispering
of the still pool we could sit down
by; of the tree of quietness
that is at hand.                               (*NTF* 26)

## The Elusive and Absent God

Yet Thomas also writes of the seeming absence of God, the *deus absconditus* that is the concern of so many mystical writers:

> Never known as anything
> but an absence, I dare not name him
> as God.                                    (*CP* 345)

Or in 'Via Negativa'

> I never thought other than
> That God is that great absence
> In our lives, the empty silence
> Within, the place where we go
> Seeking, not in hope to
> Arrive or find.                            (*CP* 220)

The emphasis is always on seeking God. God does seem to be absent much of the time and R. S. Thomas, echoing Isaiah and later Luther, thought he was a God who hid himself. Yet this hiddenness does not preclude our being able to find Him when He chooses to reveal Himself. This experience is totally different from not believing in God, for if there is no God then there is no possibility of finding Him. Thomas persevered in seeking an encounter with this kind of God, since he believed that nothing of any worth came easily and, because divinity is an entirely different entity from humanity, it provided him with the greatest challenge of his life. The hiddenness of God, therefore, draws people on like a magnet. Following Aquinas, Thomas believed God reveals Himself to people according to their ability to receive Him. So the absent God is never totally absent in Thomas's life or poetry – but there is an admission that it is only by actively searching for God that God will be found, or, more correctly, that God will disclose Himself.

Again and again Thomas finds 'a presence in absence' as he says of his dead wife. So with God:

> It is this great absence
> that is like a presence, that compels
> me to address it without hope
> of a reply.                    (*CP* 361)

There are always intimations that one comes across places where God has just been:

> It is a room I enter
> from which someone has just
> gone . . .                    (*CP* 361)

because this God is always ahead of us, 'a fast God, always before us and leaving us as we arrive' as he puts it in 'Pilgrimages' (*CP* 364). We only meet Him therefore, through our realization that He is an elusive presence, one who is seemingly continually absent. But we do see God's imprints:

> His are the echoes
> We follow, the footprints he has just
> Left. We put our hands in
> His side hoping to find
> It warm.                    (*CP* 220)

It was, of course, Thomas the Disciple who said that he would refuse to believe in the Resurrection until he obtained proof of it by putting his hand in Jesus' wounded side. But the lines also evoke the poet's fondness of placing his hand in the warm nest a bird has just vacated. Just as for the poet the only true statements about God are statements about what God is not, so too, it might appear that the only true statements about His locations are those that tell us where He is not. Thus

> We never catch
> him at work, but can only say,
> coming suddenly upon an amendment,
> that here he has been.                                          (*CP* 345)

Frustrating as that may be, it corresponds to the spiritual experience of many Christians who reach out in faith to a God who eludes them, who can never be fully grasped but who has left tantalising hints of his existence behind. Indeed, the poet compares finding God to a game of cosmic hide-and-seek. We fall, he says,

> into a presence illimitable
> as its absence, descending motionlessly
> in space – time, not into darkness
> but into the luminosity of his shadow.                          (*C* 48)

Faith reaches out to the darkness and is occasionally rewarded by glimpses of where God has been. These intimations of the divine are enough to inspire the poet to want to pursue further his relationship with God. The 'luminosity of his shadow' and the 'shadow of God's regard' are enough to sustain him in his quest.

Simone Weil believed that 'God can only be present in creation under the form of absence', suggesting that He cannot be identified with any aspect of the universe because He is the origin of all of it. So Thomas believed that when one is conscious of God's absence then paradoxically one becomes aware of His presence. Darkness and absence do not therefore necessarily imply nothingness but rather the mysterious presence of the living God as men and women try to reach out to Him. Faith is continuing to believe that one can catch those brief but encouraging glimpses of this God who is 'too fast for us'.

Crucial in this process of reaching out to God is, of course, prayer. But this too, as Thomas recognized, can be a more passive experience than one might imagine.

Praying is more of a listening than a talking – and this paying attention to God is hard work. It is waiting for God, opening oneself out to Him and spending time in His presence. Prayer is about submitting one's will to God's will, not attempting to enforce one's own will on God. And there is far more to it than reciting verbal formulae in God's presence. The poet in a radio broadcast once said that he had yet to come across a satisfactory book on prayer and often reminds us that to attain a relationship with God requires time, effort, patience and perseverance.

Thomas has no patience with the kind of person who would talk to God as if God were eavesdropping in the doorway, nor with bombarding Him with personal requests and petitions, a kind of shopping list of wants:

> I would have knelt
> long, wrestling with you, wearing
> you down. Hear my prayer, Lord, hear
> my prayer. As though you were deaf, myriads
> of mortals have kept up their shrill
> cry, explaining your silence by
> their unfitness.
> It begins to appear
> this is not what prayer is about.           (*CP* 263)

Again in another poem he explains how in the past

> It had begun
> by my talking all of the time
> repeating the worn formulae
> of the churches in the belief
> that was prayer. Why does silence
> suggest disapproval? The prattling
> ceased . . .
>                     I contented
> myself I was answering his deafness with dumbness. My tongue
> lolled, clapper of a disused
> bell that would never again
> pound on him.                           (*NTF* 83)

He writes scornfully of

> Prayers like gravel
> Flung at the sky's
> window, hoping to attract
> the loved one's
>                       attention.                    (*CP* 517)

For the most part, God does not answer prayer in either a mechanical or arbitrary way, but rather reveals Himself in personal relationships or nature. Thus in 'Folk Tale' (quoted above), the poet almost persuades himself to abandon prayer and its endless petitions. But something deters him:

> I would
> have refrained long since
> but that peering once
> through my locked fingers
> I thought that I detected
> the movement of a curtain.          (*CP* 517)

A momentary presence is glimpsed.

In the end, relating to God is about the discovery of His mercy and the growth of one's trust in Him:

> discovering somewhere
> among his fissures deposits of mercy
> where trust may take root and grow.      (*MHT* 43)

In the modern age, the advance of science has given natural explanations for things and events, which people in the past would have attributed to God's influence. Paradoxically, the poet seems to regret this passing of the age of faith in the light of more rational explanations for things and yet acknowledges that superstitious faith needed to be superseded. Even science and technology (what Thomas often calls The Machine) can reveal the presence of God:

> Not as in the old days I pray,
> God. My life is not what it was.
> Yours, too, accepts the presence of
> the machine? Once I would have asked
> healing. I go now to be doctored . . .      *(CP* 263)

'Doctored' is strikingly ambiguous. Does it mean going to be treated, cured or denatured?

The poet is saying that the world has come of age and prayer does not seem to work in the way people used to think it worked, by bombarding God with petitions and expecting Him to respond. So 'repeating the worn formulae/of the churches' is not in itself prayer; but silence is – the silence of the believer before God and God's silence before man. It is a matter of communion in which man must ask God to 'teach him to know/what to pray for' *(CP* 270), and to listen to what He might have to say in and through the encounter for

> There
> is nothing too ample
> for you to overflow, nothing
> so small that your workmanship
> is not revealed.      *(CP* 296)

That is a very different concept of God from one where the petitioner expects clear and unambiguous answers from a celestial figure. One has to be alert to the presence of God in all manner of things, and in all manner of ways. Above all, effective prayer must respond to contemporary conditions, and must never rest upon merely traditional formulae and rites. It is about nurturing a relationship, not seeking answers to a list of demands.

Because of the way R. S. Thomas has written about God's absence, some critics have questioned whether he had any faith at all. They maintain that the tortuous nature of some of the poems indicates that Thomas had really ceased to believe in God in any meaningful way and that it would have been more honest had he admitted that God did not exist rather than writing paradoxically of God's presence in absence. Yet is not R. S. Thomas addressing the question most believers face, if they are honest – whether God really exists or whether we are merely talking to ourselves when we pray? Kierkegaard, the Danish theologian, whose writings deeply influenced R. S. Thomas (and about whom he wrote two poems), posed the same questions and was, in the words of the present Archbishop of Canterbury, 'the articulator of uneasy faith and experienced living over dark fathoms'. The answer of both Kierkegaard and Thomas is that, as we pay attention to and desire this God who seems absent, He may reveal himself. And in spite of all the difficulties Thomas is, as he confesses, compelled to address God (for this is the most important relationship there is) knowing that he may not receive any kind of response. Thomas, as has already been stated, is experiencing the elusiveness and seeming absence of God, characteristic of people of faith from biblical times onwards. God is not one object among many and is not predictable. There is no guarantee of discovering him but the poet insists that God continues to reveal himself very often through the events of everyday life. Here he echoes the teaching of Jesus who invited people to see God at the heart of everyday existence and in ordinary events such as children playing in the market place or a woman baking bread. The poet concludes:

> In everyday life
> it is the plain facts and natural happenings
> that conceal God and reveal him to us
> little by little under the mind's tooling.          (*CP* 355)

It is as simple and as difficult as that.

Most Christian saints have argued that prayer is not about stridently petitioning God but waiting upon him in silence and seeing his presence in the world about us. Neither are prayers like tickets sent to God which

after a while
are returned to you with the words
'Not granted' written upon them.
I repudiate such a God.                    (*CP* 289)

That is why the poet can ask God to

Teach me to know what to pray for.                    (*CP* 270)

*I feel the power
that, invisible, catches me
by the sleeve . . .*

# Chapter 2

# God's Revelation

## (a) In Nature

Just as the poet believed God's absence conveyed His presence, so too he believed that the God who hid Himself also revealed Himself. Inscrutable and elusive though the poet found Him to be, he yet believed that God could be discovered in and through nature. The beauty God revealed in nature captured the poet's heart and was a constant reminder to him of God's awesome and mysterious workings. Whereas for many people, God was and is revealed through other people, for R. S. Thomas it was through the natural world that God was chiefly revealed. He believed that the design of nature, be it in the web of the spider, the life cycle of the mosquito or the migration of birds, revealed the beauty of the natural order and so pointed to the God who had created it.

'Look', he says, 'at the nest of the long tailed tit, with its 3000 feathers inside. Take out carefully one of the small eggs contained in it, and think of the fragile life that is developing under this miraculous shell. Nothing but? Lift your head at night and look at the heavens. Nothing but?' (*As* 131). In other words he was asking whether all this was pure chance or the work of a loving creator. In his poem 'The Moor', he writes

> It was like a church to me.
> I entered it on soft foot,
> Breath held like a cap in the hand.
> It was quiet.

> What God was there made himself felt,
> Not listened to, in clean colours
> That brought a moistening of the eye,
> In movement of the wind over the grass.
>
> There were no prayers said. But stillness
> Of the heart's passions – that was praise
> Enough; and the mind's cession
> Of its kingdom. I walked on,
> Simple and poor, while the air crumbled
> And broke on me generously as bread.          (*CP* 166)

The end of the poem draws our attention to the significance of the air crumbling and breaking on the poet like the sacramental bread of a divine Eucharist.

So he discovers God in the whole phenomenon of nature in its infinite variety and splendour:

> God is in the throat of a bird . . .
> God is in the sound of the white water
> Falling at Cynfal . . . In the flowers,
> In the wild hare.          (*CP* 43)
>
> Many creatures
> reflect you, the flowers
> your colour, the tides the precision
> of your calculations.          (*CP* 296)

But although the splendour of the creation through which God is revealed ought not to be mistaken for the Creator Himself, the natural world reveals His glory and care to the poet:

> There is a presence whose language
> is not our language, but who has chosen
> with peculiar clarity the feathered
> creatures to convey the austerity
> of his thought in song.          (*AG* 7)

He reveals Himself through the sounds and sights of the natural world. Birds are migrant creatures and so come and go, likewise God: He is not at our disposal to be continually discovered as if He were just part of the created order. God is revealed through the natural world but is not to be identified totally with that world, for He transcends it. There is, therefore, an economy about God's own chosen self-revelation:

> It is when one is not looking,
> ... that it comes.                    (*CP* 306)

But once again the human mind has its part to play. It must reciprocate and be responsive to God's revelation. The poet says that we need to be alert to be able to hear God's movement or feel the outskirts of his ways as Job puts it (*Job* 26:14), for

> I feel the power
> that, invisible, catches me
> by the sleeve.                    (*CP* 391)

So God, once again, cannot be conveniently pinned down. He is not predictable but often in and through the ordinary circumstances of life He can be discovered, or will be revealed to the receptive human being.


## Intellectual Difficulties with God in Nature

Yet R. S. Thomas is no sentimentalist or nature worshipper. He knows that his heart can be captured by beauty and that this beauty appeals to his own feelings. But beauty has to compete with truth. His heart and emotions are engaged but he is also aware of violence and terror in the natural world, and that forces him to ask vigorous intellectual questions about God's role in such violence and suffering. He cannot ignore the brutality alongside the beauty. Either

God has no part in this and is set over against another power as great or greater than Himself, or else He is responsible in some way for it, so the poet is forced to ask what place in God's love have violence and struggle? It is not so much the existence of God that is the problem for him but His nature – what kind of God is He to be responsible for such a world as this? Certain things in the natural order are outside man's control and authority:

> God looked at the eagle that looked at
> the wolf that watched the jack rabbit
> cropping the grass . . .
> He stepped back;
> it was perfect, a self regulating machine
> of blood and faeces.
> . . . It was not long
> before the creature had the eagle, the wolf and
> the jack-rabbit squealing for mercy.              (*CP* 286)

This is indeed nature red in tooth and claw with man the highest and yet the cruellest of the species. In his autobiography Thomas says that

> The sea is like a mirror – and through it you can see all the beauty and glory of the creation; the colours and the images of the clouds, with the birds going past on their eternal journey. But on using the sea as a window, an endless war is to be seen, one creature mercilessly and continuously devouring another. Under the deceptively innocent surface there are thousand of horrors, as if they were the creator's failed experiment.              (*As* 78)

This of course was the question posed to the Church by Darwin's theory of evolution in *Origin of Species*, and the poet is honest enough to admit that there are no easy answers. Moreover, it is the task of the poet to raise such questions:

> A poet is a chameleon. His privilege is to be able to change his mind and his attitude. For an honest person it isn't

possible to hold always to the same position. Face to face
with a mystery as awful as this, how can anyone be
absolutely certain one way or the other? That was Job's
problem, mute before his God.                    (*As* 79)

The world created by God seems, nevertheless, to be a
world full of predatoriness and seeming randomness.
   He poses the problem plainly in his autobiography:

> A glimpse of the blue sky through the bare trees was the
> same as looking at a stained glass window on a Cathedral.
> Looking on morning dew in the sun was like listening to
> the heavenly choir singing glory to God. The countryside
> was indispensable to his faith.                    (*As* 84)

Yet he continues:

> The weak go to oblivion. In some ways, it is quite
> terrifying. Couldn't God have done better than to make the
> earth some giant mouth which devours increasingly in
> order to sustain itself?                    (*As* 78)

And his poetry presses the same point most starkly:

> And in the book I read:
> God is love. But lifting
> my head, I do not find it
> so.                    (*CP* 297)

One of Thomas's more poignant poems portrays the
sufferings of innocent children. Can starving infants be
reconciled with a loving God?

> and one said
> speak to us of love
> and the preacher opened
> his mouth and the word God
> fell out so they tried
> again speak to us

> of God then but the preacher
> was silent reaching
> his arms out but the little
> children the ones with
> big bellies and bow
> legs that were like
> a razor shell
> were too weak to come.                    (*CP* 232)

Some critics have seen an inconsistency in Thomas's reverence for the natural world on the one hand, and its dark side on the other. For there is, as the poet admits, cruelty and waste in the evolutionary process – 'the impersonal, pitiless, beauty of Nature' (*As* 118) – but he seems, according to these critics, unwilling to draw the inevitable conclusion that there is no purpose or design behind the world, where the weakest seem to go to the wall. But is not the poet facing the same dilemma that any person of faith faces? Namely, that we live in a world of beauty and order but also of cruelty, waste, disorder and disharmony. It is an unresolved theological problem for all Christians.

## (b) In Jesus

For R. S. Thomas, there was no totally convincing answer to the seeming cruelty and indifference of a world that was meant to have been created by a loving God. He himself could only make sense of it by believing that God was, nevertheless, a God of love and that this love was revealed supremely in the person of Jesus Christ. This was not so much an answer in terms of an explanation of the cruelty and evil of the world but an answer in terms of a response to what he saw as God's attitude to the violence and terror of that world. Just as in poems when he is dealing with God's absence, God's shadow is nevertheless present, so too in poems, which deal with the cruelty and indifference of the world, the shadow of God's love in the form of the Cross illuminates the darkness. It is indeed an attempt 'to arrive at the intellect by way of the heart.' A quarter of his poems in the volume entitled *Laboratories of the Spirit* are meditations on the Cross and both his volumes *Counterpoint* and *Mass for Hard Times* deal with Christian themes, the latter dealing with the key moments of the Christian Eucharist: the Kyries, Gloria, Credo, Sanctus, Benedictus and the Agnus Dei.

Since the central message of Jesus is about loving God and loving others, and the heart of the Christian Gospel is about God's love for humanity and the world, the poet as a Christian poet struggles to convey how that love is made manifest through the person of Christ when so much of the evidence seems to point the other way. Thus in his poem 'In a Country Church' a vision is revealed as he kneels in prayer:

> He kneeled long,
> and saw love in a dark crown
> Of thorns blazing, and a winter tree
> Golden with fruit of a man's body.           (*CP* 67)

In and through the crucifixion of Jesus, the love of God shines through and beyond the crucified body. It is a vision depicted here by golden fruit – gold being the traditional colour of divinity. So a tree, which might look dead in winter, is in fact full both of golden fruit and blazing thorns. So too, on the tree of the Cross, God's love blazes out in Jesus, despite his agony and seeming abandonment.

Another poem has the same theme of this new life coming through the Cross of Jesus:

> Not the empty tomb
> but the uninhabited
> cross. Look long enough
> and you will see the arms
> put on leaves. Not a crown

of thorns, but a crown of flowers
haloing it, with a bird singing
as though perched on paradise's threshold.        (*C* 37)

Resurrection is depicted by arms putting on leaves, thorns changed to flowers and birds singing. In these images R. S. Thomas draws on his classical education but without labouring the point in any didactic way. On a Christian sarcophagus of the fourth century the cross is depicted in a triumphal wreath of laurels with birds feeding from a laurel crown. Laurels were given to victorious emperors and so the cross of Jesus is interpreted by the poet in the light of His resurrection as a symbol of hope and victory rather than of defeat. The thorns have disappeared. The poet does not mention which bird is singing but on this same sarcophagus the eagle appears as a mighty symbol for the resurrection and ascension of Jesus because that bird was said to fly highest and be able to look into the sun 'perched on paradise's threshold'.

So too, in the poem 'The Coming', God the Father and God the Son are having a conversation about the world where things have gone awry. The Son says, 'Let me go there' (*CP* 234).

The cost to God of this love is depicted in a poem about the violinist Kreisler whom the poet had gone to hear at a Cardiff recital. The poem starts with the effort and cost of the playing to the player. The disciplined effort of concentration is seen in the pulse playing in his cheek. This player is a Christ-like figure, suffering for all through his art:

who so beautifully suffered
For each of us upon his instrument.        (*CP* 104)

The poem compares the violinist pouring out himself to his audience, to God, through Jesus, doing the same for humanity and continues:

So it must have been on Calvary
In the fiercer light of the thorns' halo:
. . .
The hands bleeding, the mind bruised but calm,
Making such music as lives still . . .
it was himself that he played.

In Jesus on Calvary is to be seen God's total self-giving: a total identification with humanity. And this self-giving continues for the music lives still, for here, God is at work since, 'closer than all of them the God listened'. In another poem he depicts the crucifixion as a mystery, 'terrifying enough to be named Love' (*LS* 44). Jesus is for him not only 'Love's broken body' but also 'Love's risen body' (*CP* 359).

Suffering, violence, terror do not have the last word: God's love, through the risen Jesus, shines through. The poet does not explain how this is so, he merely states that it is so. Again in *Counterpoint*, writing of the Crucifixion, he says that

> The blood
> ticked from the cross, but it was not
> their time it kept. It was no
> time at all, but the accompaniment
> to a face staring,
> as over twenty centuries
> it has stared from unfathomable
> darkness into unfathomable light.          (*C* 40)

God's love is made manifest supremely in the Cross of Jesus and it is a love that is unchanging and continues to reassure believers two thousand years later. There is however no theological exposition of how the Cross saves humanity, or how the actions of Jesus are the actions of God.

If people want to know what God is like then they must, according to R. S. Thomas, look at Jesus because it is in

Him that God is disclosed as fully as it is possible for God to be disclosed in a human being. So although the poet believed that it was impossible to understand and comprehend God fully, yet he does not see Him as an impassible God who is unaffected by what happens in His world. In Jesus, God draws near to His world, suffers with that world, and His nature is that of overflowing love towards it. At one and the same time, God is absolutely different from and beyond His world, and yet in Jesus relates to that world in self-giving compassion and love. The action of Jesus is the action of God and the two are indivisible. The Cross of Jesus lies at the heart of it all, which means that this God suffers with and for His world and aches with it in its brokenness and tragic happenings.

God has, of course, been thought of in many different ways throughout the ages:

> We have had names for you:
> The Thunderer, the Almighty
> Hunter, Lord of the snowflake
> and the sabre-toothed tiger.
>
> . . .

God's revelation of himself however is different:

> You have answered
> us with the image of yourself
> on a hewn tree, suffering
> injustice, pardoning it.          (*MHT* 46)

It has to be admitted however that there is a certain unresolved tension in Thomas's poetic representation of God. At times He can be portrayed as a ferocious, savage, predatory being, seemingly without mercy – a passionless, feelingless, self-contained God. At the same time Thomas depicts God in Jesus as one who embraces His world with love, tenderness and forgiveness. He is not the self-sufficient, absolute monad of the Greek philosophers, unaffected by the tribulations of creation but a suffering, passionate God. Even Christian thinkers such as Augustine, Anselm and St Thomas Aquinas had tried to deny any such feelings of love and compassion to God as He was in Himself, and saw those attributes merely as those belonging to the man Jesus. Thomas makes no such distinctions. God is the God revealed in Jesus and it is God incarnate who suffers death for the world's salvation, and this God is one whose nature has always been as He is depicted and embodied in Jesus. Thus there is in 'God's side like an incurred stitch, Jesus' (*CP* 286). In other words, the suffering and pain of Jesus is felt by God because of their interrelationship. It is an interesting analogy drawing on the mutual indwelling of Father and Son as expounded in St John's Gospel.

The tension in Thomas's depiction of God however, is brought out in that same poem where the pain of the world seems to be felt by God through Jesus and yet God seems also to be depicted as laughing rather callously at the pain He Himself has inflicted, possibly deliberately, on that world.

Yet in the end there is no difference between the action of God and the action of Jesus. Thus he writes

> This Christmas before
> an altar of gold
> the holly will remind
> us how love bleeds.                    (*Res* 47)

There is no systematic explanation of how this is so, just a poetic assurance that that is the case.

Thomas tries to elaborate on God's involvement in the mess and pain of the world. Although at times He is portrayed as the omnipotent being who can do what He wants, as He wants, at other times He seems a limited, vulnerable God as disclosed in the person of Jesus, who cannot save the world from the effects of evil and tragedy but who deals with it by being involved in its pain and shouldering it with the human race. He cannot make pain and tragedy disappear and so has limits to His omnipotence. He cannot even save Jesus from the Cross and compares Him to

> God's fool, God's jester
> capering at his right hand
> in torment, proving the fallacy
> of the impassible, reminding
> him of omnipotence's limits.                    (*C* 36)

In this, R. S. Thomas echoes Dietrich Bonhoeffer who in his letters from his prison cell wrote that

> God is teaching us that we must live as men who can get along very well without him. The God who is with us is the God who forsakes us (*Mark* 15³⁴). The God who makes us live in this world without using him as a working hypothesis is the God before whom we are ever standing. Before God and with him we live without God. God allows himself to be edged out of the world and on to the cross. God is weak and powerless in the world, and that is exactly the way, the only way, in which he can be with us and help us.

The paradox is striking. It is what St Paul means when he says God's strength is revealed in weakness not in power and that it is in the crucified Jesus that God is really to be found.

Yet Thomas does not work out a systematic view of the atonement or of suffering or indeed of any other religious theme. His concerns are not those of a systematic theologian. He is concerned to link God and the Cross of Jesus so that the nature of the God cannot be understood without that link. In the poem 'Cain', and in response to the world's tragedy, God is heard to say that

The lamb was torn
From my own side. The limp head,
The slow fall of red tears – they
Were like a mirror to me in which I beheld
My reflection.                                    (*H'm* 15)

How that is so, the poet leaves to the reader to work out and through.

The dictionary definition of *Counterpoint*, the title of one of R. S. Thomas's volumes, is 'the technique of involving the simultaneous sounding of two or more parts or melodies or to set in contrast'. It sums up much in Thomas's verse. There are no easy answers, just the exploration of questions, statements and counterstatements interweaving. Elaine Shepherd in her book on the poet says that he explores the gap between observation and revelation – the world as he sees and feels it and the world as the Christian faith claims it to be. Thus he explores at one and the same time, like the simultaneous sounding of two or more melodies, the absence and presence of God, the paradox of suffering and love and the being and nature of God. God seems far removed from humanity and gives the impression of showing no great interest in it and yet He is a God who has drawn near in Jesus and whose presence is with us. So too, God seems capricious and uncaring:

God took a handful of small germs,
sowing them in the smooth flesh. It was curious,
the harvest: the limbs modelled an obscene
question, the head swelled, out of the eyes came
tears of pus.                                    (*CP* 286)

Yet He is also a God of grace who comes to us in mercy:

> When we are poor
> and aware of the inadequacy
> of our table, it is to that
> uninvited the guest comes.                    (*C* 62)

It reflects his own admission that an honest poet has
to reflect what he sees and it is not always possible to
hold a consistent or even logical viewpoint. He himself
said that he became a priest because although the world
of nature was often cruel, he was, nevertheless, impressed
by the evidence of design within it; and that the symbols
of Christianity had the essence of truth about them,
especially the Cross, since all love involved suffering and
sacrifice.

Some critics have alleged that Jesus is far less
prominent in Thomas's poetry than God and that is true.
They have deduced from this that his faith was not a
Christ-centred faith and that he found the Old Testament
more congenial than the New. Yet, although there are
bewildering contradictions in his poetry about God's
nature, and constant agonising about that nature, his
theology is in the end a Christocentric one. He is honest
enough to face his own doubts and lack of belief although
sometimes it is hard to know whether the questions he
raises are his own questions or questions he raises on
behalf of others. He is not a theologian who tries to
expound in a systematic way a doctrine of God, Jesus, or
major Christian themes such as Salvation, the Atonement
and the Resurrection. He makes no attempt to explain how
God's love is revealed in Jesus, just that it is. It is
something he takes for granted and comes back to again
and again in spite of all his doubts. For the poet, if people
want an insight into the nature of God, they can only find
it in the crucified Jesus, for in Him God's total self-giving,
vulnerable love for the world is revealed. The essence of
divine being is not power but love. As Rowan Williams
puts it, 'God looks into the crucified human face to see

who He is, to see Himself in the centre of the world's suffering'; or as another former Archbishop of Canterbury, Michael Ramsey, once put it: 'God is Christlike, and in Him is no Unchristlikeness at all'.

*He was too big to be nailed to the wall*
*Of a stone chapel, yet still we crammed him*
*Between the boards of a black book.*

# Chapter 3

# Further Theological Insights

**R.S.** Thomas was a religious poet, but he was no deist. He was a Christian poet, even if a troubled and controversial one. His poetry is shot through with Christian themes, allusions and images; the Cross and Resurrection, the bread and wine of the Eucharist figure prominently in his work. There are religious undertones and insights in a large number of his poems even when he is writing on secular topics such as modern art, Wales, the machine, or the landscape, since for him religion deals with both the real world and ultimate reality. Poetry is an attempt to explore them imaginatively and artistically. Nevertheless, Thomas admitted that there were truths in other religions and that Buddhism, Hinduism and Taoism were appropriate and true in their own cultural contexts. He believed that since Christianity was the religion of Europe, it was through Christianity that God had revealed Himself to the West (*As* 106). That may not seem like a whole-hearted endorsement of the Christian faith, nor his description of central Christian doctrines such as Resurrection and Incarnation as only metaphors. For him Christianity was the presentation of 'Imaginative truth' rather than historical or literal truth. He recognised that there might be different paths to God for only God Himself embodies the whole truth.

Some have been perturbed by the honesty and brutality of his explorations, even his unorthodoxy. He saw his vocation, however, as asking difficult questions, no matter how unorthodox they seemed, and at times his poetry is an attempt at shocking his readers so that they are forced to think through the implications of their faith for themselves. Thus, for example, he can turn roughly on God, challenging him sardonically:

> I believe in you, the almighty
> who can do anything
> you wish . . . Rid therefore
> (if there are not too many
> of them), my intestine
> of the viruses that against
> (in accordance with? Ah, horror!)
> your will are in occupation
> of its defences.                    (*MHT* 12)

That is a concept of prayer he dismisses constantly in his poetry, but it shows how difficult it is to reconcile a God of love and goodness with the tragic things that happen to people.

He says that on the Day of Judgement he would have a great number of things to say to God:

> storming at him,
> as Job stormed, with the eloquence
> of the abused heart.                    (*CP* 331)

But when he rails against God, Thomas is in line with both the Bible and Christian tradition, where there are numerous examples stretching from the Psalms through the Book of Job, to Jesus in the garden of Gethsemane, and where the individuals concerned are honest enough in their prayers 'to look God in the eye and tell him how it is' to quote one recent theologian. When he eventually meets God face to face, the poet says he will continue the approach he has adopted in his prayer-life of venting both his anger and distress against and to the Almighty.

Some people have been shocked by the way the poet pours forth his wrath against the Almighty and articulates his doubts in His presence. Yet many of the Psalms ask

God why He seems to have abandoned His world. Psalm 22, for example, pours scorn on God for sitting comfortably on His throne whilst the psalmist is scorned by men and despised by people. Job, having lost his livelihood, status, health and family refuses to accept the conventional wisdom of his day, that these are somehow God's punishment for his sins. He pleads his innocence and in his grief and anger against God accuses Him of being a tyrant and a sadist and even compares God to an animal, for God is tearing him apart as an animal would his prey – 'Thou dost hunt me like a lion, and again work wonders against me'.

Thomas said that what he tilted against was not God Himself but what he regarded as false ideas about Him:

> I am really being derisive about men's ideas of God . . . I believe in God, I'm trying to show how people sometime attempt to pin down this, this Being who's not a Being. A lot of my work is ironic, which possibly some people wouldn't always get. (*AWR* 40)

So he writes:

> We have over-furnished
> our faith. Our churches
> are as limousines in the procession
> towards heaven. (*C* 37)

He also chastises the Church for trying to pin God down too neatly:

> They laid this stone trap
> for him, enticing him with candles,
> as though he would come like some huge moth
> out of the darkness to beat there. (*CP* 349)

The Church to his mind had tried to define God too carefully. He himself, however, admitted that he was not always consistent in what he wrote. He was not, as we have said, a systematic theologian trying to expound the Christian faith but a man who in his poetry wrestled with certain personal insights into his own faith when they seemed to be at variance with conventional wisdom or beliefs. That enabled him to explore various aspects of faith and doctrine and to admit to doubt, uncertainty and discomfiture. He was willing to face the difficult questions, which threaten belief and was not afraid to admit the fragility of his own faith. He admits that sometimes:

> . . . Walking
> time's sea I have faltered
> like Peter, unable
> to believe you had arms
> to sustain me.                              (*Res* 23)

He says that the church has sometimes tried to restrict the sovereign freedom of God:

> . . . History showed us
> He was too big to be nailed to the wall
> Of a stone chapel, yet still we crammed him
> Between the boards of a black book.         (*CP* 117)

For him, God and Jesus are bigger than our thoughts about them for although Holy Scripture testifies to people's experiences of God, and thoughts about Him, that God, because He is God, cannot be restricted to those thoughts and experiences. Continually Thomas comes back to the question of who can really fathom God's mind. He suggests that all our doctrines of God and the Trinity are provisional and in a sense superficial. We all tend to make God in our own image and by so doing confine and restrict Him. For Thomas, God is infinitely bigger and more mysterious than we can ever think or even imagine as mere humans. There can be no tidy solutions as far as faith is concerned. He followed Wittgenstein in believing that 'what is ragged must be left ragged'. Organised religion, he believed, had too great a desire to tidy things up. For him religious belief was essentially precarious and provisional. Too often it wanted to claim too much and often wanted to give answers when there were more questions to face. It is obvious from his autobiography that he kept up his theological reading since he refers to the work of Bishop John Robinson of *Honest to God* fame, who also questioned conventional images about God.

Again Thomas is doing no more when he thinks in this way than some of the biblical writers. The prophet Isaiah reminds God's people that God's thoughts and ways are different from theirs. God in the book of Job answers Job's accusations against Him by asking him where he was when He fashioned the earth and asks him 'Shall a faultfinder contend with the Almighty?' (*Job* 40$^2$) and Job is forced to admit that 'he has uttered what he did not understand' (42$^3$).

Thomas often brings the reader up short with his original and fresh interpretation of the Christian faith. He says of the mediaeval philosopher, Roger Bacon, that he:

> . . . dreamed on in curves
> and equations
> . . . he saw the hole
> in God's side that is the wound
> of knowledge and
> thrust his hand in it and believed.     (*CP* 354)

Here he draws once again on the image of the risen Christ offering to let Thomas put his hand in His side. Thomas refuses but Bacon takes up the challenge and believes. By implication the poet raises the place of faith and doubt in the believer's life, but at the same time, by implication says that faith and scientific knowledge are not incompatible. So too in 'Pieta' alluding to the cross of Jesus at Calvary he has an arresting image of

The tall Cross,
Sombre, untenanted,
Aches for the Body
That is back in the cradle
Of a maid's arms.                                    (*CP* 159)

The Cross aches for the body of Jesus as Mary aches when Jesus' body is taken down from it and is laid in her arms as it once was at His birth.

These images and thoughts are the result of deep contemplation and prayer, as he says:

. . . after long on my knees
in a cold chancel, a stone has rolled
from my mind, and I have looked
in and seen the old questions lie
folded and in a place
by themselves, like the piled
graveclothes of love's risen body.        (*CP* 359)

Just as the stone was rolled away in the Garden of Gethsemane so a stone has been rolled back in his mind, enabling him to see more clearly that the answer to many of his doubts and questions are to be found in the risen Jesus.

But he also has poems which attempt to see things from God's viewpoint not man's. In these God discusses with man his own existence and power. Thus in 'Rough' he deals with the question of creation, and in 'Amen', redemption. In 'The Hand' God wrestles with the hand He has made, afraid of the way it misuses its power, for it destroys rather than builds and is tempted to undo God's creation. But reminiscent of Jacob wrestling with God, the hand wrestles but God lets it go, but without His blessing, fearful of the harm it will do. God, although He refuses in this poem to bless His creation, has nevertheless given it a freedom over against Him to go its own way and

> . . . to bellow our defiance
> At you over the grave's maw. (*C* 51)

It is no wonder that Søren Kierkegaard was the poet's favourite philosopher since he too was honest and unconventional enough to ask radical questions. R. S. Thomas belonged to what is known as the apophatic tradition believing that it was impossible to pin God down and almost impossible to make any absolute statements about Him; if one did then one had also to make another qualifying statement even if it seemingly contradicted it. Silence in the presence of God was the right approach and yet the poet could not remain silent with all his questions, so that here too he is full of contradictions.

Although a Christocentric poet, he admitted in conversation that there were no real means of knowing for sure what Jesus had actually said or indeed of understanding his message after this length of historic time. In any case, that message was delivered in a different language from ours and faced all the perils of translation. The culture and background of Jesus' world were also totally different from ours and for the poet there was a large poetic element in the teaching of Jesus, hence the challenge of it. In all of this Thomas is reflecting the view of New Testament scholars that Jesus 'is God's metaphor and speaks to us so' (*AWR*). Yet in his last volume *Residues*, published after his death, in a poem entitled 'Watching' he says that God watches His world

> from behind the cross that is
> the astigmatism in his vision. (*Res* 11)

Yet in spite of this essentially Christocentric approach he referred to the Resurrection as metaphor and pondered in his autobiography as to where, if it happened, this resurrection would occur. He seemed to imply that resurrection was essentially a western idea tied in to the continual rebirth of nature through the seasons, something which did not happen in the tropics. Related to all this is the question of where, if anywhere, the soul goes at death.

In a moving tribute to his first wife published in *Residues* he writes:

> She, too:
> here, gone. I know when,
> but where? Eckhart,
> you mock me . . .
> Immortality, perhaps,
> is having one's
> name said over
> and over?                                      (*Res* 25)

It was Eckhart who said that at death there was no need for the soul to go anywhere and so in this poem Thomas's dead wife lives on in his remembrance of her. She is a presence in absence. So too in 'The Morrow', in response to the same persistent question about the soul at death:

> There is no need under a pillarless
> heaven for it to go anywhere.                  (*Res* 58)

That seems to imply that this life is all that there is.

In a broadcast in 1972 he said that 'eternity is not something over there, not something in the future; it is close to us, it is all around us and at any given moment one can pass into it. Life and death, the eternal and the temporal, the human and the divine perhaps form a continuum, mysterious but compelling'.

Yet not long before he died he was reading a book on Time and Eternity. I tentatively asked him how he felt about death. 'We came from God and go to God' he replied, 'that was good enough for Augustine and it is good enough for me. For He who created us will at the last receive us'. That is an eloquent testimony of his deep faith at a critical time, as was the deeply reverential way in which he received the sacraments. In his autobiography he said that it was up to God whether he became someone in another world.

Thomas summed up his own position in that 1972 television broadcast when he said that his work as a poet had to do

> with the presentation of imaginative truth . . . and in presenting the bible to my congregation I am presenting imaginative interpretation of reality. By imagination I mean the highest means known to the human psyche of getting into contact with ultimate reality; imaginative truth is the most immediate way of presenting ultimate reality to a human being and we call it God.

Despite his radical and unorthodox thinking, Thomas was conservative and conventional when it came to liturgy. He disapproved totally of westward celebrations and preferred to have his back towards the congregation leading it in worship towards the transcendent of God. For him a westward celebration devalued the mystery of God and seemed as if the Church was setting out its wares to sell to people to try to attract them to faith. In a poem called 'Bleak Liturgies' he says:

> We devise
> an idiom more compatible with
> the furniture departments of our churches.          (*MHT* 59)

Churches seemed to him to have become like commercial enterprises and by seeking to modernise the language of the liturgy had devalued the sense of the otherness of God in worship. Having the priest face people in presiding at the Eucharist seemed to him more akin to selling groceries than leading people in the worship of God.

He preferred the poetic language of the 1662 Prayer Book to modern alternatives. Modern liturgies in his view did not aid a sense of devotion or transcendence:

> Instead
> of the bread the fraction
> of the language.                    (*MHT* 59)

In that respect he was more of a product of the Anglo-Catholicism of his theological College than perhaps he realised, although it could be argued that his liturgical approach is in line with his theology, that the living God has to be treated with respect and reverence. Yet despite everything he believed that the 'verities remain':

> the chalice's
> ichor; and one crumb of bread
> on the tongue for the bird-like
> intelligence to be
>                      made tame by.          (*C* 37)

He belonged to the George Herbert tradition of Anglicanism – not only in his devotion to country parishes, and in his writing of religious poetry but also in his distaste of what he regarded as too much 'mateyness' in religion. He believed that God was the only goal worth pursuing – a God who was full of mystery, darkness and splendour, for the poet knew that:

> somewhere beyond the eye's
> range he maintained
> his fullness.                      (*Res* 19)

The Puritan divine Richard Baxter defining George Herbert's qualities said of him that 'heartwork and heavenwork make up his poetry. Herbert speaks to God as one who really believes in God.' The same can be said to be true of R. S. Thomas.

R. S. Thomas in his life and in his poetry had a hunger for the living God. This God may have been elusive, and believing in Him not always easy, but the sense of attempting to form a relationship with the God who transcends us and all our thoughts about him is a constant theme in his poetry. God exists and we as humans attempt to respond to that being, difficult as it may be. He believed that one had to carry on working at that relationship even though one may not feel the presence of God very often. As he put it 'To learn to distrust the distrust of feeling . . .' (*CP* 353). And in line with classical orthodoxy, Thomas believed that this God was elusive because He did not want to force His being upon us. If we are to form a relationship with Him, we must do so voluntarily:

> To yield to an unfelt pressure that, irresistible in itself,
> had the character of everything
> but coercion? To believe, looking up
> into invisible eyes shielded against love's
> glare, in the ubiquity of a vast concern? (*CP* 353)

God is present to His world and is concerned about everything and everyone in it but does not bludgeon us into belief for

> As I had always known
> he would come, unannounced,
> remarkable merely for the absence
> of clamour. (*CP* 283)

'Absence of clamour' is different from real absence. God's approach to His world is unobtrusive, even ambiguous because He wants to elicit a response not demand one.

In and through what happens to us, in and through the natural world, God is revealed so that we can say that:

> coming suddenly upon an amendment
> that here he has been. (*CP* 345)

God is present to His world but does not force Himself on it. People have to open their eyes to discern Him.

Thomas ends his introduction to the verse of George Herbert with these words: 'it has the simplicity and gravity of great poetry. It is a proof of the eternal beauty of holiness'. It rings true of his own poetry as well. He speaks to our generation since he deals with the seeming absence of God, the concept of a God of love in a world full of tragedy, the meaning of prayer and eternal life, and the significance of the suffering of Jesus in it all. As he himself put it in a radio broadcast, 'if talk of the eternal is to have any sense, it must be seen in the illumination it provides or fails to provide for the temporal facts of human existence'. Or, more poetically:

> . . . He sings to me
> in the chain-saw, writes
> with the surgeon's hand
> on the skin's parchment messages
> of healing . . .
> . . . I listen to the things
> round me . . .
> speaking to me in the vernacular
> of the purposes of the One who is.              (*CP* 426)

But the God of R. S. Thomas speaks to him in the mess of life as well as in its glories, which is why his faith survived. As he put it:

> You are there also
> at the foot of the precipice
> of water that was too steep
> for the drowned: their breath broke
> and they fell. You have made an altar
> out of the deck of the lost
> trawler whose spars
> are your cross.                                 (*CP* 351)

There is no explanation to the tragedies of life but here Thomas implies that God is shouldering them alongside His world and that that is what he does at Calvary.

The literary critic and scholar, A. E. Dyson, says that it was Thomas's poems which drew him back to faith in 1966, and not the dogmas of religionists. 'It was the voice of this poet, speaking out of dereliction, which called back towards blessing'.

That holds true for many people. For this poet, at one and the same time, to misquote the hymn, had 'faith, belief but questioned how'.

Paradoxically, R. S. Thomas who has been accused of pessimism and lack of faith is able to give heart to the modern church, which at times is inclined to despair about its future as fewer people come to worship. He reminds it of its long history and how faith continues even when the institutional church is in crisis. The fortunes of that church ebb and flow but because God exists people still seek Him, perhaps in different ways from their forefathers but they still do so. What is asked of the church at a time such as this is to remain faithful in waiting upon God.

> . . . These very seas
> are baptised. The parish
> has a saint's name time cannot
> unfrock . . .
>        . . . people
> are becoming pilgrims
> again, if not to this place,
> then to the recreation of it
> in their own spirits. You must remain
> kneeling.

          (*CP* 282)

# Bibliography and Abbreviations

*As*    R. S. Thomas, *Autobiographies* (Phoenix, London, 1997). Translated from the Welsh by Jason Walford Davies.

*AG*    *Agenda* A Tribute to R. S. Thomas, Vol 36, No 2, 1998.

*AWR*    *Anglo-Welsh Review* 74 (1983) R. S. Thomas talks to J. B. Lethbridge.

*BHN*    *Between Here and Now* (Macmillan, London, 1981).

*C*    *Counterpoint* (Bloodaxe Books, 1990).

*CP*    R. S. Thomas, *Collected Poems* 1945–1990 (Phoenix, London, 1990).

*H'm*    *H'm* (Macmillan, London, 1972).

*LS*    *Laboratories of the Spirit* (Macmillan, London, 1975).

*MHT*    *Mass for Hard Times* (Bloodaxe Books, Newcastle upon Tyne, 1992).

*NBF*    *Not that he brought Flowers* (Rupert Hart-Davies, London, 1969).

*NTF*    *No Truce with the Furies* (Bloodaxe, Newcastle, 1995).

*PBR*    R. S. Thomas (ed.), *The Penguin Book of Religious Verse* (Penguin Classics, Harmondsworth, 1963).

*Res*    *Residues* (Bloodaxe Books, Northumberland, 2002).

*WV*    R. S. Thomas, *A choice of Wordsworth's Verse* (Faber and Faber, London, 1971).

*The Cloud of Unknowing* (Classics of Western Spirituality, Paulist Press, New York, 1981). J. Walsh ed.

'Meister Eckhart, Sermon 42' in Oliver Davies, *The Rhineland Mystics* (SPCK, London, 1989).

*Echoes to the Amen* (*Essays after R. S. Thomas*) ed. Damian Walford Davies. (University of Wales Press, Cardiff, 2003).

*R. S. Thomas Conceding an Absence*, Elaine Shepherd (Macmillan Press, 1996).